The YouTuber's Handbook
Second Edition

Copyright © 2018 by Oliver Leopold.
All Rights reserved. This book or any portion thereof may not be reproduced or used in any manner whatsoever without the express permission of the publisher except for the use of brief quotations in a book review.

Second edition.

ISBN-13 978-1979496933
ISBN-10 1979496935

This book is in no way affiliated with YouTube, Google, or Alphabet, Inc. All opinions are my own with no influence by any platforms, affiliates, or third parties. YouTube is a trademark of Alphabet, Inc. Please visit our "Fair Use Statement" page for more information.

Pictures are copyright by their rightful owners. Sources are found in the footnotes. If the owner has a conflict, please contact the email below.

For questions or comments:
Oliver Leopold
handbook@oliverleopold.com

A very special thanks to:
Alexander Brown, Eric Drinkard, Jon Prosser, Mary Leopold, Paul Groseclose

Table of Contents

Introduction 1

Thumbnails 3

Monetization 7

Quality Content 10

Sponsorships 13

Equipment 18

Video Editing 23

Collaborations 27

YouTube Partner Program 30

Live-Streaming 33

Cards / End Screen 36

Getting More Subscribers 40

Analytics 43

Social Media 51

Set Design 53

Conventions 55

Monetization Outside YouTube 57

Consistency 60

Closed Captioning 62

Intro's 65

Banner Design 68

Longer Videos 71

MCNs and Networks 73

SEO 76

YouTube Space 79

Demonetization 81

Encouragement / Discouragement 84

Affiliate Programs 87

Copyright 90

Responding to Comments 93

Benefit Levels 96

YouTube Studio App 99

Introduction

More and more people are making it big on YouTube, and more and more people are having a lot of fun doing so. Whether you want to be a YouTuber as a career, or just as a hobby, you need to start somewhere. Sure, YouTube seems easy, but be prepared for a pretty bumpy ride. It'll take a while, and there's no one big secret to reveal, but there are some tricks and tips that will be helpful to you.

YouTube is a very complex platform. You may just see a website where you can watch all sorts of videos, but a lot happens behind the scenes. Ever wonder how they pick recommended videos for you? Or how they can handle 300 hours worth of content uploaded every single minute? Well, yeah, it's a little complex.

The YouTube Platform actually does pick favorites, and the algorithm to do so changes every single day. That said, there are some specific ways to stay in-the-know and make sure the platform favors you. This is *The YouTuber's Handbook*, a second-edition handbook to all things YouTube.

There are a few ways of reading this book. The obvious way is "cover to cover." You can start at the beginning, and end at the end. This is a great crash course. If you know *nothing* about the platform and don't know where to start, that may be ideal. But what if you've already started your channel? Well, in that case, you may choose the chapter selection method. Head over to the table of contents and pick a chapter that you want to learn more about. Most chapters are pretty short, but they do cover all the basics of the subject.

Once you've read the chapter, read it again. If this is your personal copy of the book, feel free to circle things and underline to make sure they stand out to you. Now, you can go back to this chapter later and easily see what you found important. Once you're done, go back to the table of contents and pick another chapter. Also, if you see a little number at the top of a word (like this[1]), it means there's more information at the bottom of the page corresponding to that number. Usually, if I'm referring to a specific channel or website, I'll put the link there.

Compared to the first edition, this book is much more in-depth and advanced. In fact, this edition is about three times as packed with words and covers much more complicated topics.

I'll be your guide through this handbook. My name is Oliver and I'm glad that we'll be taking this journey together. I have a YouTube channel of my own (called Oliver Leopold) and love helping people start their own channels. When I wrote this specific edition, I was only 15 years old. Whether you're my age, older, or younger, I hope you enjoy *The YouTuber's Handbook* and learn something. See you at the end! Good luck!

P.S. Keep a look out for future editions. Since YouTube changes so frequently, I hope to write more.

---

[1] Here is where you will find the corresponding information.

Thumbnails

Thumbnails are one of the most important things about creating a successful video. The thumbnail is the small image shown before you click on a video so people know what to expect. Once your video is uploaded to the YouTube platform, YouTube uses high-tech algorithms to create three different thumbnails.

Here's what the algorithm does: it looks at thumbnails from very popular videos and marks them as "positive examples." Then, it takes random pictures from the video and marks them as "negative examples." When you upload your video, it will go through all of the frames and find three pictures that the algorithm believes best resembles a "positive example."

Sure, sometimes one of those three thumbnails is a winner, but usually not. A lot of the time, a thumbnail will need additional text or photo editing. In my thumbnails, I usually find a frame from the video of me making a happy face. I then get this picture, blur out the background, add any text/pictures and am done.

Study Tips!

I sometimes get frustrated when the thumbnail of a video doesn't resemble any frame from the video at all. The point of the thumbnail is that the viewer knows what to expect when they click on the video. Sure, you can exaggerate the thumbnail and add a lot of emojis and do a dramatic edit, but start with a frame from the video.

A good thumbnail does all of these things:
1. Gives the viewer an accurate idea of what the video will be about.
2. Gives the viewer an accurate idea of the setting of the video.
3. Is very easy to read, and stands out even if you look at it for a second.
4. Draws attention to the video, making the viewer excited and eager to watch.

Let's try an example. Jack is making a video about his favorite studying tips. He found a great frame from the video where he is smiling. Here are some tips to make this frame even more clickable.

His first step is to blur the background. Blurring the background is a super easy quick trick to help the thumbnail. You want the thumbnail to focus on the subject, which is Jack. The blur lets us control what the viewer sees in this quick glance. Many different softwares can help you do this, but I just use Photoshop.

Finally, we add text and a picture (I like to use an emoji). Now, even if viewers don't read the title of the video, they know what the video is about. One tip about pictures and text is that you need to make sure they are big enough. Some thumbnails are going to be displayed on a tiny phone, so make sure the words pop out and are easily readable.

One thing to note: your account must be verified to upload custom thumbnails. And no, I don't mean the little check mark by your name. All you need to do is go to youtube.com/verify and give YouTube your phone number. At that point, you are allowed to upload custom thumbnails and unlock a few other features.

You can upload your thumbnail from the YouTube Studio app, from the video manager, or from the upload page.

Monetization

So you think you're ready to make money from your YouTube channel? There are a few ways to make money from your videos, but the easiest is YouTube Monetization. This just means that YouTube will put advertisements on and around your videos, and then pay you. As of February 2018, if you have less than 1,000 subscribers and less than 4,000 watch-time hours in the past year, you are not eligible for monetization. **That said,** you can still set up monetization, and your account will be reviewed once you hit these milestones.

First, make sure you verify your account. Simply go to youtube.com/verify and provide them with a working phone number. Next, head to your Creator Studio, click Channel and find "Status and Features." Under monetization, click Enable. Follow the steps and accept the YouTube Partner Program Terms (if you are under 18, it is important that you follow these steps with an adult, as it is a large legal document that is to be taken seriously). Next, you need to sign up for AdSense. AdSense is the software for publishers (YouTubers, bloggers, etc.) to get paid for ads put on their content. Creating an AdSense account takes time and needs to be set up properly.

Find the YouTube Help article entitled, "Set up an AdSense account for payments"[2] and follow those steps.

Make sure you set up AdSense properly and wait for the account to be approved. It can take anywhere from a couple of days to months, but AdSense should notify you of any problems. Please know that AdSense is strict about only having one account, so **do not** create multiple AdSense accounts (or they all could be shut down).

Now, you need to set up your videos for monetization. You have the choice of which videos to enable or disable for monetization. In your Creator Studio, click Channel and then Upload Defaults. Here, find Monetization and select "monetize with ads." You can now select your ad formats. Selecting all of them will provide you with the best opportunity to make money. Now, whenever you upload a video, it will automatically be monetized. To monetize past videos, head over to your Video Manager, select all of your videos, and then click Actions and then Monetize.

Once you hit 1,000 subscribers and more than 4,000 watch-time hours in the past year (or if you already have), your account will be reviewed for monetization and you can begin making money.

Now that you know *how* to monetize your videos, let's learn more about the process. In September 2017, the YouTube platform went through the *apocalypse*, where advertisers refused to buy ads because they were being placed next to inappropriate content. YouTube's response was to use an algorithm to figure out if a video was inappropriate, and if it was, "demonetize" it, or make it so the creator couldn't make money.

Many creators who relied on YouTube for their income were devastated because videos were being "demonetized" and they couldn't make any money from them. Sometimes, this

---

[2] https://support.google.com/youtube/troubleshooter/7367438?hl=en

would happen with a perfectly PG video. Many months later, YouTube hasn't fixed anything, but they are trying their best. You can now submit an appeal (if your video gets significant views) and they are working hard to resolve this problem. Advertisers are happy, but creators aren't.

That's not the only way your monetization can be taken away. Let's talk about copyright (discussed even more in later chapters). Say, for example, you drew a painting. But then, Sam walks in, makes a copy of the painting, and sells it. Sam was making a ton of money off of your painting. That's not fair!

This happens on YouTube with music, video segments, and pictures. YouTube finds a way to protect copyright owners (like the painter). If you use someone else's music in your video, there is a chance that the monetization will be taken away from you, and all money made from the video will go to them. The other option is for them to take down the video altogether.

But how much money will you make? Well, that depends. A lot. There's no way to know exactly. Most people rely on what a popular analytics website, Socialblade, has to say. That said, they offer ranges like "$558.9K-$8.9M." Those ranges are too big and not reliable. Additionally, it doesn't take demonetization and YouTube Red into account.

CPM, or cost per thousand, is an advertising term for 1,000 ad impressions (clicks, watching long enough, etc.). This CPM changes per ad, but an average is a $2.50 CPM. One ad impression roughly equals one view, but if they have ad-block, you don't get any impression.

After that, YouTube takes 45%— ouch! So, for every thousand views, you can expect to earn about $1.62. That said, you could get lucky and find an advertiser that will pay a lot more CPM. With a really big channel, the CPM will increase because an advertiser will pay more to be showcased by that video. For large creators, they could expect upwards of a $5 or $6 CPM, but that can be hard to accomplish.

Quality Content

Making quality content is a fundamental requirement for long-term success on the platform. And when I say "quality content," I don't mean to say that you need a nice camera or other nice equipment. Sure, equipment is important, but not as important as some other factors. In this chapter, we will explore what you can do to make your content the highest quality possible.

Let's start by discussing your equipment options. I know I just said it was unimportant, so let's just get it out of the way. I would like to preface this again by saying: you don't need a nice camera or lighting to start your channel. Don't buy a camera before you know how you enjoy making videos. An expensive camera will increase the quality of the content in a literal aspect, but it's not about the equipment, it's how you use it. If you have high-end devices like an iPhone or a nice webcam, you should definitely use that. iPhones and flagship Android devices are great starter tools and will give you everything you need until your channel grows. To learn more about different equipment and different price points, look at the "Equipment" chapter. If you buy a camera off the bat, though, you may never see that money again, nor do you know that you really enjoy making videos or if you would like to pursue becoming a YouTube creator.

Regarding equipment, though, you can get the best quality by utilizing tools like a tripod (or propping the camera on something stable), lighting (natural light works perfectly), and proper video editing. While editing the video, try to take out as many unnecessary uses of "um" and "like" as possible. Additionally, try to learn as much about your equipment as possible so you know how to properly utilize it.

The quality of your content also relies on your ideas and how you execute them. An idea is of high quality if it's original, you know how to execute it well, and fits into your channel's category or niche. Making original content is challenging, I know. Brainstorming ideas and trying to figure out what people haven't done is near impossible but isn't the only way to make original content. If everyone is doing a certain challenge, try to tweak it a little bit to make it your own, whether that's a new rule you add or you just add your personality. Let's use the "try not to laugh" challenge as an example, a challenge where someone is shown a series of videos and does anything they can to not laugh. Instead of making a "clone" of the thousands of other challenges, you can do something like adding a punishment that fits the niche of your channel. For example, a makeup channel could blindly apply some makeup every time they laugh. Remember: if you can't come up with your own ideas, find a way to put your own touch on other's ideas.

"Selling out" is a big concern for content creators and audiences- and you need to be cautious. "Selling out" is when you trade your beliefs or normal content for a financial reward. An example of this is if you are making dedicated sponsored content back-to-back and abandoning your regularly scheduled videos. There are many ways to avoid this, but the main ideal to follow is just to simply not be greedy. Remember that, unlike a job, YouTube is not a stable source of income. At any time, your viewers could stop watching and you'd stop making money.

With this in mind, try to make sponsored content as small of an interruption as possible and make an effort to incorporate it. Never do anything out of the ordinary that you wouldn't regularly do for money. Not only will your audience get upset with you, but you will regret it later.

Sponsorships

For some YouTubers, sponsorships can yield very large amounts of income and help legitimize their channel. A sponsorship is like an advertisement. A company will pay a YouTuber for a shout-out or a whole video dedicated to their company—and they'll pay a lot. Though sponsorships are annoying for viewers, they sometimes fit into normal content and are not too bothersome.

To get sponsorships, you have a few options. Let me preface this by saying that if you have less than a couple thousand subscribers, it's going to be difficult. My favorite way to get sponsorships is a website called FameBit[3]. FameBit, which is now owned by YouTube, allows companies to post different sponsorship offers and creators to post proposals. Additionally, you have a guarantee because everything is monitored through FameBit.

The next method of getting sponsorships is a cold-call. This option is definitely the hardest, as it requires you finding a random company, contacting them, and hoping for a response. It

---

[3] www.famebit.com

has actually worked a couple of times for me, but only after I sent hundreds of emails. Don't expect a response, because they come very rarely. I personally recommend emailing, simply because it's easier. Here's a really nice format that you can use as a template:

Dear [Company Name],

My name is [my name], and I have a YouTube channel called [channel name]. The channel has over [subscribers] subscribers and [lifetime views] views. I would like to talk to someone on your team about a sponsorship on my channel. What that means is that I would shout-out or make an entire video about your [product/service], and you would compensate me for the advertising. The final charge would be less than traditional advertising, and it would be beneficial for both of us.

Insert "personal area" where you discuss:
- Why you like their product/service.
- Why your audience would like their product/service.
- What experience (if any) you have dealing with companies and sponsorships.
- What they would get out of doing a deal with you.

If you are a minor: Make sure to say that in your letter. Don't let them figure it out themselves. Also, CC your guardian on the email and insert the following: "I have CC'd my [mom/dad/aunt/uncle/etc.], [their name], since I am a minor. If you would like to communicate with them alone, please reach out."

The final method for finding a sponsorship is when the company reaches out to you. Obviously, this is the easiest because you skip many of the initial steps. Throughout the negotiation (this applies to the cold call, too) you need to figure out how much you are going to charge. There's no easy way to calculate this amount, so I recommend using Social BlueBook[4]. They have a lot of really cool creator tools, but my favorite is the "Platform Valuation" tool. Simply connect your YouTube account, adjust the parameters, and they will tell you the right price to charge. They will compile that information and some basic demographics that you can pass on directly to the company.

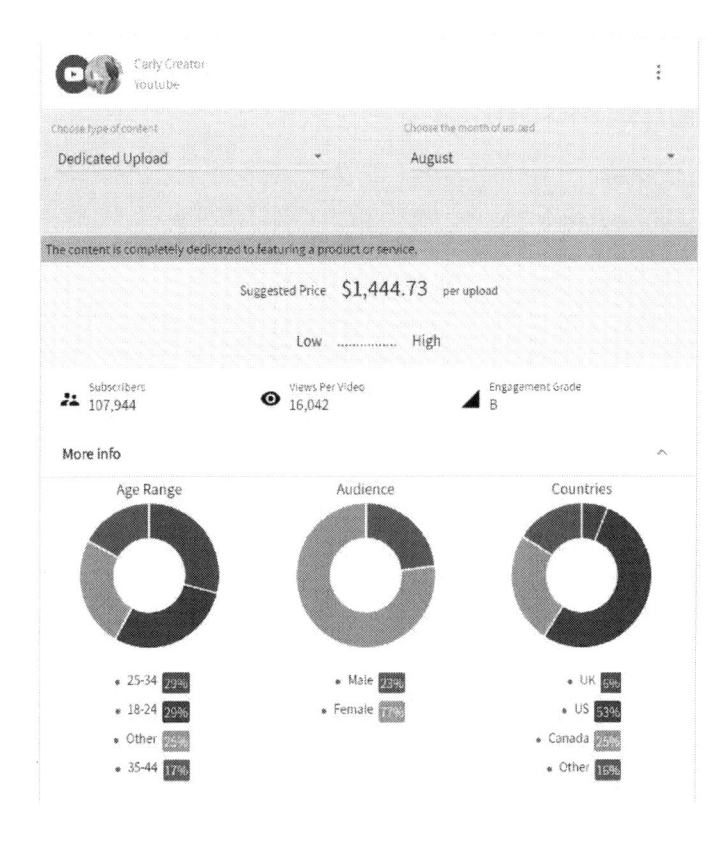

Carly Creator
Youtube

Choose type of content: Dedicated Upload
Choose the month of upload: August

The content is completely dedicated to featuring a product or service.

Suggested Price **$1,444.73** per upload

Low .... High

Subscribers: 107,944
Views Per Video: 16,042
Engagement Grade: B

More info

Age Range
- 25-34　29%
- 18-24　29%
- Other　25%
- 35-44　17%

Audience
- Male　23%
- Female　77%

Countries
- UK　6%
- US　53%
- Canada　26%
- Other　15%

Now that you and the company have agreed on a price, you need to make the video. Whether it's a shout-out or a full video, make it a professional and high-quality video. If the company hasn't paid you yet, they could decline the video. Upload the video as "unlisted" when you are done, and send the link to the company. Let them review it before you publish. Listen to them, and make any changes that they request. Make sure to add proper links in the description. Now, here's the big thing: the United States law requires you to disclose any sponsored content. How can you do that? At the beginning of the video, just say, "I would like to thank [company name] for sponsoring this video." In addition, put "#ad" or "#sponsorship" near the top of the description. Lastly, go to the video edit page (click "edit video" if you are on the watch page). Select "advanced settings" and scroll down.

Content declaration

✓ This video contains paid promotion such as paid product placement, sponsorships or endorsement ⓘ

✓ Help me inform viewers of paid promotion by adding a disclosure to this video. Additional disclosures for this video may be required under applicable laws ⓘ

Always select the first box if the video is sponsored. By selecting the second box, a small card will show up during the first ten seconds of your video.

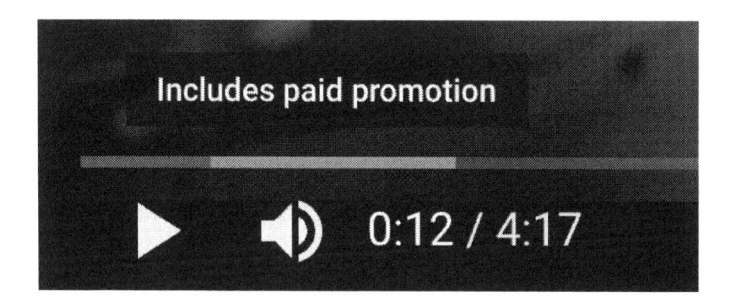

You need to make a strong effort to tell your audience the video is sponsored because the FTC (Federal Trade Commission) requires that the viewer doesn't need to "look for it." Remember that sponsorships are very rewarding, but you need to do them just right.

Equipment

For people who are making content on YouTube and love video production, equipment can be one of the most fun things to think about. I always like to have the best camera, best microphone, etc. In this chapter, we're going to be talking about the best physical equipment to use for YouTube. The four main categories are cameras, microphones, lighting, and accessories.

I have compiled a list for people that have a budget and are very serious about YouTube. If you are just starting out, I recommend using a smartphone. Any phone made in the last few years has comparable quality to a starter camera. In fact, a smartphone has much better quality than low-tier cameras. Just a quick disclaimer: this is a book, which means when new technology comes out or prices change, it doesn't update.

Nikon D3200 - The Nikon D3200 was the first DSLR I ever owned. The quality is great and you can't go wrong. With a lens, it will cost around $400, which is definitely worth the price. Keep in mind that the LCD screen doesn't flip out, so you won't be able to see yourself while recording.

Canon T6i - The Canon T6i is an incredible camera to shoot on. Though I've never used one, I've seen the footage from one of them and it's really great. With a lens, this camera will run you about $600, but it'll last you a long time. Additionally, it's Wi-Fi enabled so you can transfer footage from the camera to your phone or tablet without a cable.

Canon G1 X Mark II - Whether you're a vlogger or just in need of a more compact camera, the G1 X Mark II is incredible. The screen flips up, so you can see yourself and the built-in microphone is great. It has great image stabilization and costs $650.

Canon EOS 80D - If you have a little bit of a bigger budget, the EOS 80D is a great camera for you. Coming in at $1,300 with a lens, the quality is simply stunning. The pullout screen is also really great to have.

Rode VideoMic Micro - If you are recording with a phone, and the phone still has a headphone jack, the Rode VideoMic Micro is a great choice. It easily plugs into your phone and improves the sound quality greatly. For just about $50, you can't go wrong.

Rode VideoMic GO - I owned this microphone for many, many years and it's really nice. For under a hundred dollars, it sounds great and doesn't require a battery. It's powered by the camera, so it can never die. This microphone will mount on top of most cameras.

Blue Yeti - The Blue Yeti microphone is a little bit different than the others I've shown. It's big, heavy, and requires to be plugged into a computer. That said, almost every YouTuber has owned one in their lives. The Yeti only costs $100 and sounds great. You could place it slightly out of the frame in a video, or use it to record voiceovers or sound effects. Making a podcast? Great for that, too!

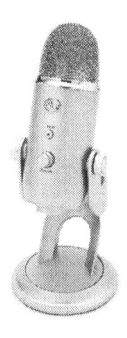

The Sun - The best way to light your videos is the sun. It's bright, free, and looks very natural. Recording outside or in a room with big windows on a sunny day is sometimes all that you need.

Fancierstudio DK2 - Umbrella lights are the only kind of lights that I used for the first few years of my YouTube career. They're super bright, easy to assemble, and not too expensive. This kit comes with two of them and costs under $40. When you're ready to record, just turn them on and you get a nice bright glow to your videos.

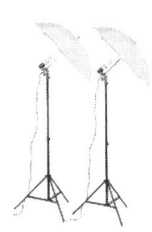

Neewer 14-Inch Ring Light - For just about $125, you can get everything you need to get started with a ring light. This includes all of the mounts and filters, too. Ring lights are perfect for makeup videos or anything where you're talking close to the camera. They're a great source of light and put a white ring in your eye. Additionally, you can mount your camera on the inside of the ring.

SD Card(s) - I'm not going to recommend a certain brand because most SD Cards are the same, but make sure you have multiple on hand. Most cameras use them to store pictures and videos, and the fill up really quickly. To avoid needing to delete footage before you transfer to your computer, buy a few 32GB SD Cards that cost about $10 each.

External Drive - I really don't like deleting videos and footage, even after I post them to YouTube. In case I need a certain clip or the whole video in full quality (YouTube turns down the quality a little bit), it's nice to have my own copy. External Drives are great because they can store thousands of gigabytes of data and work like a flash drive. I recommend the Western Digital drives, which are about $50 for one terabyte (1,024 gigabytes).

Tripod - Simply screw your camera into the top of a tripod to keep it still and steady. Owning and using a tripod is always a great idea. I use the Fancier FT717, which is about $100 and is super professional. If you just care about a steady shot, AmazonBasics sells a few nice tripods for under $20.

Video Editing

Video editing is one of the most important things you can do when it comes to producing a good video. Without video editing, almost no video on YouTube would be very watchable. Sure, it may seem funny to watch bloopers, but watching someone sit and wait to think of proper phrasing, repeating a sentence many times to get it right, and just being boring is not fun.

A big question for a YouTuber (big or small) is: what video editing software do I use? This question is very justified as there are dozens of options, accomplishing very different things at very different price-points. I strongly believe that until you are financially stable and ready to upgrade, you should stay with built-in or free software.

iMovie[5] is a great example. As long as you have a Mac (or iPhone, iPad, or iPod Touch), you can use iMovie for free. Sure, in the professional and sub-professional world, iMovie is frowned upon but is a great beginner tool. You can add background music, make cuts, add pictures, and more.

---

[5] www.apple.com/imovie/

The best thing about iMovie, in my option, is the gateway to Final Cut Pro[6]. Final Cut Pro (FCP) is one of the two most used video editing software in the professional world. Though it's expensive, coming in at $300, it's well worth the price. If you are fluent in iMovie and ready to upgrade, FCP is a perfect option. It's only available on Mac, but is fast, has countless features, and has a ton of support. The best thing about FCP is that when you buy it, you get all of the updates for free.

But what if you don't have an Apple Device? Well, if you are looking for a mobile (phone/tablet) solution, there are many options on the Google Play Store. One of the best is Adobe Premiere Clip[7] (and is 100% free). That brings us into the Adobe Suite. Adobe Creative Cloud is the most used suite when it comes to content creation. The package includes Photoshop, Premiere Pro, and more. That said, the package comes in at $50/month for individuals and $20/month for students and teachers (only valid for one year).

Premiere Pro[8] is the most professionally used video editing software. It was used to make movies like Gone Girl, Deadpool, and Hail Ceaser. One of the best things about Premiere is that it is cross-platform meaning you can use it on a Mac or Windows computer. Sure, it'll cost you a pretty penny, but if you are doing anything professional, it is well worth it.

If you have a Windows computer, what could you use for free? A software called Lightworks[9] has your back. It's completely free but acts like a paid software. It is also available for Mac and Linux. I personally haven't used it, but after looking at the feature list and online reviews, it looks very promising.

---

[6] www.apple.com/final-cut-pro/

[7] http://www.adobe.com/products/premiere-clip.html

[8] http://www.adobe.com/products/premiere.html

[9] www.lwks.com

So now that you have found your editor of choice, how can you edit? Well, it's pretty simple. Video editing is unique because of how it changes with different projects. For example, if you are trying to edit a comedy video, your editing needs to reflect that. You can cut a video and add in subtitles and music to complete a joke or make comedic timing perfect. If you are doing a makeup video, proper titles will help viewers understand what you are working with.

For YouTube videos, the main things you'll be doing with an edit are chopping, music, text, overlay pictures.

Chopping: Chopping—or trimming—a video is incredibly important. On YouTube, you are trying to keep a viewer watching for as long as possible. To do this, cut out breaks in speech or words like "um" and "like." Chopping a video is also crucial to attaching separate clips. If you're making a vlog, you need to figure out where to chop a clip and how to transition into the next one. You could do a jump cut (no transition), a fade/effect transition, or a video montage as a transition.

Music: Background music is very important to help the viewer stay engaged. A lack of background music could be important to send a certain message. This music is very hard to find, as you need to find tracks that are copyright-free and that you can use. Ever since I visited VidCon 2016, I have used one tool for all of my background music, Jukedeck[10]. It uses artificial intelligence to generate music. Basically, you put in the kind of vibe, instruments, length, and it will provide you with a soundtrack. This soundtrack is free for you to use (as long as you give them credit), and can never be regenerated by another user. Therefore, you'll be the only one using this song. No more reusing the same song everyone uses.

---

[10] www.jukedeck.com

Text: Though not super important to the video editing process, text can help display information that you forgot to/did not say in the video itself. This can be your social media information at the end of the video, or a correction to something you said in the video. For example, if you are making a video about a new phone and say it has an 8-hour battery when it actually has a 10-hour battery, you could correct that on-screen instead of re-recording the segment.

Overlay Pictures: Placing pictures and videos over your main track can dramatically change the professionalism of the video. You'll see this all around YouTube. You could show a picture of someone you're talking about, or play a video (without sound) on-top of your track to show something. All video editing software will allow this, though some will limit how many layers (overlays) you can have.

Collaborations

A collaboration, or collab, is a great way to make new friends and make really fun content. A collab is simply when two or more content creators work together to make content. There are three types of typical collabs that we're going to review in this chapter. Additionally, we'll discover the benefits of making collab videos.

The first type of collaboration is definitely the most common. In this collaboration, you and your friend make a video together for each of your channels. This is great for when you're both in the same geological location and have similar channel categories. When making this type of collab, make sure you plan the video out beforehand, because it can be the hardest part. Lastly, make sure to put a link to the other video in the description and advertise it. You will see this type of collab very often on YouTube because it is so much fun to do and very easy.

The second type of collab is best for people who aren't in the same geographic location. You both make a similar video (like "celebrities I've met") independently. Then, at the end of the video, you shout-out the other person. This kind of collab isn't as fun to make, but you still get to spend time coming up with ideas with the other person. If you've met someone online and can't physically get to them, this is your best option.

The last type of collaboration is not a full video, but just a small piece. It doesn't necessarily require that you're in the same geological location but can work if you are. You will see this a lot in animation videos, but they're everywhere. In animation, you could have a friend record themselves saying a line or making a sound effect. A popular animator, theodd1sout[11], does this frequently to support his friends and the animation community on the internet. If you need a clip, sound, picture, or any help, remember that content creators are the most qualified to help you.

There are many perks that come from making collaboration videos. The first is very obvious: it's a lot of fun. You get to go through the video-making process with your friend! The next perk is getting new subscribers. Since the video will have more views (coming from your friend's channel), you need to convert them into subscribers. The easiest way is asking viewers to subscribe at the end of the video. Also, put a similar video on the end screen. This way, they'll watch more of your videos and conversion rates dramatically increase.

Figuring out who would be a good partner for collaboration can be tricky. Let's say that you make makeup videos. You would want to do a collaboration with someone in the same bubble: makeup, hair, or style. Sure, it's possible to hybrid two very different categories, but it's much more difficult. Remember that the goal is for your friend's audience to watch their video and then immediately go and watch yours. Make sure that both audiences would naturally do this. Finally, don't **ever** collaborate with someone if you think they're boring or can't appreciate their content. It's fine to say "no" to someone, always be professional and polite.

---

[11] youtube.com/theodd1sout

In the "sponsorships" chapter, I discuss FameBit[12] and how the website can help you get sponsorship deals. What I didn't mention is that it has an entire section just for collaborating. If you're looking for some help, you can make a post and other creators will respond.

---

[12] www.famebit.com

YouTube Partner Program

The YouTube Partner Program (YPP) helps creators make money off of YouTube without the need of a network or MCN (learn more about MCNs in the chapter entitled, "MCNs and Networks"). In August 2007, YouTube started playing advertisements on videos, and just four months later, the YPP was announced. The YPP was started as a way to pay video creators and to encourage them to use the YouTube platform.

These days, there are many perks to joining the YPP, and they extend beyond just monetization (making money from ads). As long as you have more than 1,000 subscribers and more than 4,000 watch hours in the last 12 months, you are eligible for the program. This view threshold is because YouTube manually reviews each application, so a threshold filters out spam or very new channels. Additionally, you need to be based out of one of the 94 currently supported countries.

Even if you just created your YouTube channel, you can complete the steps to becoming a member of the YPP. Then, once you hit the threshold, your account will be reviewed. If you are a minor, please make sure you complete all of these steps with your guardian. There are important legal documents that should not be overlooked.

These steps are the same as the steps in the "Monetization" chapter, but the YouTube Partner Program covers monetization and many other topics that will arise. First, head to your Creator Studio. Select "channel" and then "status and features." Where it says "monetization," click "enable." Now, just follow the steps to agree to the terms and conditions of the YPP. Next, you need to set up your AdSense account. AdSense is Google's solution for paying content creators (YouTubers, Websites, etc.) for serving ads on their site. Once your channel has been reviewed and you have completed all of the steps, you are officially part of the YouTube Partner Program. Congrats!

The YouTube Partner Program gives you access to some really cool features. Most YouTube Partners have access to Super Chat, a live-stream donation tool. Whenever your live-streaming, it lets your viewers donate money and attach a comment. This comment is pinned at the top of your chat for a certain amount of time. This is a really incredible feature because it allows you to make a lot more money from live-streaming, and the income flows into the same place as your ad revenue.

Select YouTube Partners have access to a new YouTube feature called "sponsorships." This feature is YouTube's reaction to websites like Patreon, where viewers get perks for monthly donations. Like Super Chat, this feature can be done outside of YouTube, but it's nice to have it baked right in. With the sponsorship, your fans can pay monthly for features like a special badge in comments, custom emojis, and sponsor-only posts. If you're just entering the YouTube Partner program, I wouldn't recommend enabling sponsorships. Some viewers will think that you're "selling out," and with a small audience, it's unlikely you will find people who are willing to contribute $5+ per month for your content.

It doesn't seem like that big of a deal, but my favorite part of the program is the support. Usually, if you need help or have a YouTube question, you need to go to a forum or ask a friend. If you're part of the YouTube Partner Program, you can actually send YouTube an email and they'll help you out. Question about copyright, monetization, or your channel? Send them an email, and they'll reply within a day or two. I have personally used this a few times and it's incredible. There are some limitations as to what they can help you with, but basic questions and requests can be addressed.

Becoming a YouTube Partner is a write of passage for creators. You start the process of being recognized by YouTube and start climbing the ladder to fame. It's never too early to apply to the program since they'll wait for you to hit the threshold before reviewing your application. There's no downside, and it's an incredible opportunity.

Live-Streaming

Live-streaming is one of the best ways to make your audience stronger and it's very fun. Personally, I love doing a quick live-stream from my phone just to chat with my audience. It's an easy way to chat with the people who watch your videos and make a more genuine connection with them. Live-streaming to YouTube is super simple and you can get started really quickly.

First, you need to make sure you have a verified phone number before you start streaming. Do this by going to youtube.com/verify and following the on-screen steps. In the creator studio, go to "Live-Streaming" to enable, or select "create a live-stream" on a mobile device. On a mobile device, it's super easy to get going. Select some options, snap a thumbnail, and go live! This is the easiest for a quick stream, but you can also live-stream from a computer.

Live-streaming from a computer is a bit more complicated but much more professional. The steps require more technical knowledge, so I'm not going into them with too much detail. You need to find a live-streaming software (I recommend OBS since it's free). Set up your scene, and input the credentials found at the bottom of the YouTube page. Edit the details on the page and go live from your software.

I like to live-stream ten minutes before posting a new video. People will join and then they can watch the video. It can increase buzz about the video and then engagement. Another thing I do is give three random people from the live-stream a shout-out in the video's description. Therefore, there's an incentive for turning on notifications and watching the live-stream.

Don't expect too much ad revenue from live-streaming. For example, if 20 people come in the stream (which is a significant amount), you are making the same as about 20 views. With a live-stream, viewers need to be in the right place at the right time. That said, I always upload an archive on the live-stream so people can watch it later. This way, I can get a little more ad revenue off of the stream.

YouTube is not the best place to live-stream, but for growing an audience it's very important. Everyone tells me I should be streaming on Twitch, but my audience is on YouTube and that is where I'm trying to improve engagement. I don't want two small followings on both platforms; I want the majority of my following on one platform.

Adding a moderator to the live chat is very important. Have a friend or a fan that you trust moderate the chat to keep it positive and spam-free. A moderator can put a user in a time-out or ban them altogether if they are ruining the fun in chat. For me, I try to have a discussion with the chatroom, and a few people can easily ruin that discussion with spam. (Pro tip: make sure your moderators are not censoring innocent viewers.)

One newer feature is "super-chat." This allows viewers to donate money and get a comment pinned to the top of the chat for a certain amount of time. I know it seems crazy, but some viewers will literally *pay you* to see their comment or to just thank you for being a great creator. The more money a viewer contributes, the longer it will be at the top of the comment section for everyone to view. No matter the length, you will be able to see all super-chats in your live-stream dashboard. All contributions will be added to your AdSense.

Cards / End Screen

Cards and end screens are relatively new features and represent ways to increase engagement with cross-platform support. A card is an informational link, text, or poll that shows up in the top right corner of a video. You can select the exact time and the data. Some great uses for cards are promoting other videos or external links. An end screen is a view that you can add to the last five to twenty seconds of a video. In the end screen, you can add links to videos (which appear as thumbnails) or channel icons (for easy subscription). In this chapter, we are going to review the perks of these tools and how you can properly implement them.

For some end screen and card features, you must be a YouTube Partner. Once you have uploaded your video, you are ready to start editing your end screen and cards. Let's start with the end screen. Simply select the "End screen & annotations" tab at the top of the video editor page. You will automatically be brought to the frame 20 seconds before the end. On the right side, you can select the "Add element" drop-down box. Here, you have an option for four types of end screen elements.

First is the most common: a video or playlist. This is pretty straightforward, and you can promote a video or playlist of yours or someone else's. Next is the subscribe element. This element adds your profile picture to the end screen. A viewer can click the picture to view the subscribe button or go to your channel. Similarly, the channel element works with somebody else's channel. Finally, the link element allows you to select a link to an approved website. There are three categories for approved websites: associated, merchandise, or crowdfunding. A link will automatically be checked to see if it is a merchandise or crowdfunding website. If you would like to choose a unique link, you must associate it as a website you own/manage. You can do this in your advanced account settings.

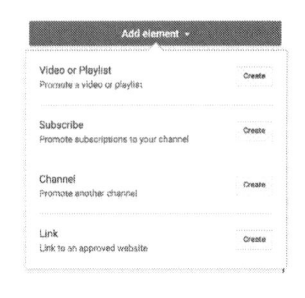

Once you've added all of your elements to your end screen, you can arrange them on the video and on the timeline. When created, the elements are placed in random spots. Move them around in your desired arrangement. Additionally, elements appear on the timeline at the bottom of the page. Drag around the element to indicate when it should appear. Ideally, you want all of the elements to appear at or around the same time. Finally, select the "preview" switch to see how it looks!

Cards can be shown throughout the entire video and are great if you are referencing a separate video. You may add up to five cards per video, and they can all be viewed when clicking the "i" in the top right corner of a video. Head over to the "cards" section in the video editor page. You will notice that the setup is very similar to the end screen editor. They are almost identical, except for their behavior and slight differences to content.

Like end screens, you are able to make a card for any video, playlist, or channel. Additionally, the options for creating external links are identical. Two cool additional features are adding a poll and donations. By adding a poll, the viewer can click on the card and vote quickly. This option is great for predictions or getting an opinion. Setting up a poll is incredibly straightforward and simply requires a question and some responses. A donation card allows you to raise money for a registered non-profit. Simply enter their name and the message to your audience. Finally, move the cards on the timeline just like on the end screen editor.

Both of these similar tools can help overall engagement. For example, linking a similar video in the end screen can result in a higher conversion. Higher conversion equals more views and a higher chance of subscription. Polls can help you get insight from your audience (and are just a lot of fun). Additionally, if you're doing a collaboration, it's a great way to give proper credit to the other channel(s) at the end of the video.

If I can remember, I try to add a "best for viewer" video element to every video. This way, YouTube will automatically find a related video of mine that the viewer hasn't yet seen. It's like the suggestion features, but it's inside the video frame. Then, through YouTube Analytics, I am able to view my clickthrough rate of the different end screen and card elements.

Whenever you're uploading a new video, try to set it to "private." Then, when it's done processing, you are able to set up your cards and end screens properly. When you are finished, just set the video to "public" and you are done. Remember that the most significant views come in right after the video was posted, and you should not leave those views without cards or end screens.

Getting More Subscribers

Everyone focuses on subscribers as a metric of how successful your channel is. In reality, average video views mean a lot more. That said, the subscriber count is an easy number to look at and means something. Just remember: subscribers help your channel grow, but other statistics mean a lot more. Now let's learn how to get more subscribers.

There are many ways to get *bad* subscribers that I would strongly discourage. Buying subscribers is one of the worst things a small channel can do to get started. Why? Not only will it set you back a pretty penny, but it's against YouTube's policy. Sure, there is a small chance that you would be caught, but YouTube could terminate your account if they really wanted (and you would not get a refund). The bigger reason is the quality of the subscribers. You are paying for some random bot to subscribe to your channel. You are not paying for likes, comments, and views. Therefore, you will still be getting few views on every video, and people will get suspicious. The point of a subscriber is that they will engage with your content, but you would not get any engagement this way.

Another way people get *bad* subscribers is doing "sub-for-sub." There are many apps and websites (along with the

YouTube comment section) that manage the process of "you subscribe to me, I'll subscribe to you." When people do this, they are usually repeating this process with hundreds—sometimes thousands—of people. Sub-for-sub rarely yields long-term subscriber relationships, and people usually stay subscribed for a while and then unsubscribe because you are spamming their subscription box.

So now you know how to get *bad* subscribers (that aren't even worth your time), so how do you get *good* subscribers? Well, that is a little more difficult. You are going to be frustrated with my answer since there really isn't one. There are many methods you can use to help you get subscribers, but there is not a surefire way.

The easiest way to get new subscribers is simply by posting content. When you have more content, the chances that some random person will come across your videos are much higher. And if you have more people watching your videos, you have more people getting the chance to subscribe. It's like a shop. If you put a shop in the middle of nowhere, you will get no customers because there is no foot traffic. But if you put the same shop in the middle of a busy city, you have more people walking by and more people potentially buying something. To convert a viewer into a subscriber, make sure the video is the highest quality possible, and you ask people to subscribe at the end.

Joining online communities can also help find genuine subscribers. YouTube has different online forums (read about them in the chapter entitled "Benefit Levels"). By participating in the community, answering questions, and staying engaged, other people from the forum may click on your profile, visit your channel, and subscribe. **Do not** advertise yourself, but just be a part of the community. Not only can this help you find subscribers, but it can help you find other members of the YouTube community to work with.

My last tip is to promote to people in real life. I've been at numerous events where I was talking to people that I didn't personally know. When I was talking about myself, I subtly mentioned my interest in video production and making YouTube videos. At the end of the conversation, I give them the name of my channel, and voilà! Since they have formed a personal relationship with you (meeting you in real life), they have a higher chance of not only subscribing but viewing and engaging with videos.

Analytics

Understanding YouTube Analytics is one of the most important skills a creator can have. Analytics can help you understand what you're doing right and wrong. Analytics can get very complicated, so in this chapter, we're going to go through a few views and try to analyze them. These views should help you best understand how to read a vast variety of analytic views on the dashboard. (Pro tip: to view your analytics dashboard, just go to youtube.com/analytics.)

All of the data from the next few pages are simulated in order to help you get the best idea of how analytics work.

Average view duration
Minutes

3:35

Watch time
Minutes

10,400 ▼

Watch-time and average view duration work hand-in-hand with each other. Watch-time is how many minutes of your videos have been watched in the time range. The time range for this data is currently set to "last 28 days," so the graph is watch-time over these 28 days. If three people watch your videos for five minutes each, your watch-time would be 15 minutes. The down arrow indicates that the watch-time from the last 28 days is less than 28 days before that. Average view duration is simply how long an average person watches your video.

Top geographies
Watch time

United States (79%)
United Kingdom (11%)
Canada (2.7%)
India (2.4%)
Philippines (0.9%)

Gender
Views

● Male (83%)
● Female (17%)

Traffic sources
Watch time

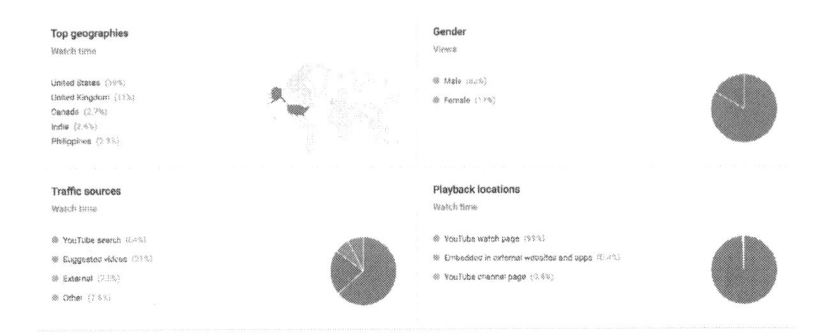

● YouTube search (64%)
● Suggested videos (21%)
● External (7.1%)
● Other (7.9%)

Playback locations
Watch time

● YouTube watch page (89%)
● Embedded in external websites and apps (10.4%)
● YouTube channel page (0.4%)

It's important to understand how to read each of these panels. In bold, you can see the name of the statistic, and you can see the metric below that. For example, "gender" and "views." The data you can see is showing information about what genders are watching your videos, sorted by the number of views per gender. Therefore, the data is saying that 83% of my views comes from males. In "traffic sources," it is sorted by "watch-time." Therefore, 64% of my watch-time comes from YouTube search.

These four panels tell us a lot about the channel. For example, you can see from this mockup that the typical traffic is a male from the United States watching from the YouTube watch page and discovered the video via YouTube search.

YouTube ad revenue ↓	Estimated monetized playbacks	Playback-based CPM	CPM
$1.51 (31%)	47	$32.07	$25.98
$1.45 (30%)	583	$2.48	$2.45
$0.87 (18%)	4	$216.89	$173.52
$0.61 (13%)	34	$17.90	$9.98
$0.18 (3.7%)	14	$12.60	$8.40
$0.09 (1.9%)	1	$89.50	$89.50
$0.08 (1.6%)	2	$38.45	$38.45
$0.01 (0.3%)	26	$0.51	$0.36
$0.01 (0.2%)	7	$1.64	$0.76
$0.01 (0.2%)	1	$8.48	$2.83

This data, which can be found under "Ad rates" shows how much money you make per video and what the CPM is. If you remember, the CPM is how much money you get per thousand impressions (or ad views). It can range very dramatically for random reasons. "Estimated monetized playbacks" is the best estimate of how many ad views there were. One view doesn't equal an ad view, because of skippable ads, devices that can't show ads, AdBlocker, and YouTube Red[13]. You are only making money off of these monetized playbacks. As we can see, some videos are getting tremendously high CPMs. That said, those are also ones with very few monetized playbacks, so there is not enough data to get a very average CPM. The $216 CPM is only realistic for a couple of views.

---

[13] YouTube Red revenue shows up elsewhere

Device type	Watch time (minutes) ↓	Views	YouTube Red watch time (minutes)	YouTube Red views	Average view duration
Mobile phone	7,340 (59%)	4,720 (61%)	247 (72%)	148 (69%)	1:33
Computer	2,858 (23%)	1,716 (22%)	41 (12%)	35 (16%)	1:39
Tablet	1,736 (14%)	1,095 (14%)	51 (15%)	31 (14%)	1:35
TV	221 (1.8%)	80 (1.0%)	4 (1.2%)	2 (0.9%)	2:46
Game console	220 (1.8%)	135 (1.7%)	0 (0.0%)	0 (0.0%)	1:37
Unknown	66 (0.5%)	38 (0.5%)	0 (0.0%)	0 (0.0%)	1:44

The "devices" tab is some of the most important data you can receive. We can see that "mobile phones" are responsible for 61% of the views. Since we see phones are such a big deal for this channel, we need to make sure we are making on-screen text big enough and thumbnails readable. Phone screens are not too big, so make sure they are properly optimized. Going along with the screen size, we can see that TV users will watch a video for one minute and 13 seconds longer than phone users. We might want to investigate if this channel's videos favor a larger screen, because our goal should be to properly optimize the content for all viewers, or we could see some problems.

End screen element type	End screen elements shown	End screen element clicks ↓	Clicks per end screen element shown
Best for viewer	17 (55%)	2 (67%)	11.76%
Video	4 (13%)	1 (33%)	25.00%
Channel	3 (9.7%)	0 (0.0%)	0.00%
Subscribe	5 (16%)	0 (0.0%)	0.00%
Most recent upload	2 (6.5%)	0 (0.0%)	0.00%

The end screen is a very powerful tool to help engagement and direct viewers to more videos and subscription. This statistic, under "end screens" and "end screen element type," shows us which end screen element is most successful. "Clicks per end screen element shown" is the click rate of that element. Therefore, we can see that a direct video on the end screen becomes the most successful.

Subscription status	Likes ↓	Dislikes
Not subscribed	145	33
Subscribed	8	0

"Likes and dislikes," sorted by "subscribers" will show you this information. It is challenging to act on but something that is very interesting to visualize. As you can see, it shows me that viewers that are subscribed have a higher chance of liking the video than those who are not. With that said, this statistic teaches us a great lesson about survey size. It's like an election. If we were to only ask one city in the middle of Texas who should be president, we would get a different result than if we asked the entire country. The bigger the survey size, the more accurately the data reflects everyone. For "not subscribed," we see a survey size of 178 (145+33), but for "subscribed," we only see a survey size of 8. Therefore, it would not be fair to conclude that this data is completely accurate until we have a larger survey.

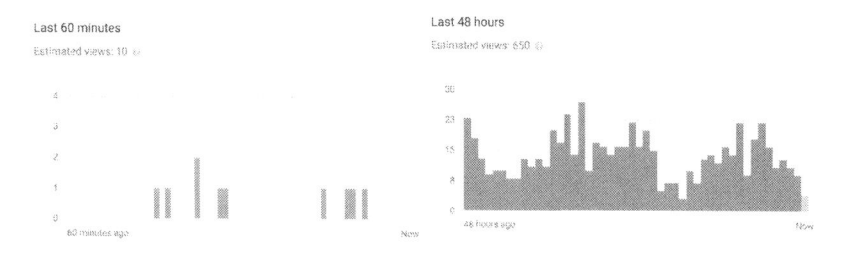

Last 60 minutes	Last 48 hours
Estimated views: 10	Estimated views: 650

Real-time analytics are the newest way to track your views without waiting for the next day. This data is very helpful if you release a new video to see the immediate response. Real-time analytics update every ten seconds and provide you with views of the last 60 minutes and the last 48 hours. Additionally, you can split them into categories by device, operating system, and geography. The first couple days are when most of the views for a video usually roll in, so it is great to see where they are coming from and how many there are. Data from the dashboard is always more accurate than data on the watch page.

Social Media

For many content creators, YouTube is the go-to place for their audience and to raise popularity. That said, integrating other social media is incredibly important for building a brand and engaging your audience. In this chapter, we'll be looking at the best social media platforms to accomplish this.

Twitter is a very important tool to grow your brand because it allows you to update your audience with short status updates. Not only is is important to post yourself, but you will also want to retweet and reply to your followers, retweet other content creators, and follow people back. Make sure that you are posting about any live-stream, new videos, or updates. While you're trying to gain popularity, open up your DMs (direct messages) to get private messages from fans and followers. When that gets too chaotic, you can simply turn it off. On Twitter, you will find a tremendous amount of support from your community and you will be able to meet many new and interesting people.

Instagram is another very popular social media app that is used by content creators, but it is not always the go-to. Unlike Twitter, there is less of a community and it is not advisable to post more than once per day. Instagram allows for sharing of great pictures and can correspond with other content creation, but it's hard to respond to comments and have your audience feel heard. Instagram Stories, on the other hand, is a great place to promote videos and any important announcements. With Instagram Stories, you are free to post "behind the scenes" content of your life multiple times per day.

Snapchat[14] used to be a great tool for creators, as they were the first to offer "stories," and any user is able to connect a link to a story. It also allowed, if you wanted, to be able to respond to your followers via private message. Sure, the community isn't as open as Twitter, but it's a middle ground between Twitter and Instagram. That said, certain apps like Snapchat have taken involuntary and unfortunate steps to reduce story views and make it less of a hub for creators.

Twitch has always felt like a competitor to YouTube, but did you know that you can use them hand-in-hand? Twitch is a live-streaming website mostly for gaming; so if you're not a gamer, Twitch probably isn't for you. If you are, though, you can use Twitch and YouTube together! When you are streaming on Twitch, your audience is mostly people who enjoy video games. And if they're watching your stream, they most likely enjoy your content. All you have to do, then, is convert these Twitch viewers into YouTube subscribers (which isn't too hard). Make sure to add links to your YouTube channel around the stream, and utilize chatbots to post it from time-to-time. On your YouTube channel, add links to your Twitch account. Now, you've cross-promoted and YouTube subscribers will become Twitch viewers and Twitch viewers will become YouTube subscribers.

---

[14] Please note that this paragraph was written at the beginning of 2018, after a series of large updates that greatly decreased Snapchat's popularity.

Set Design

Designing a background or set for your video can sometimes be the easiest thing you do. That said, I've also spent countless hours figuring out the ideal location for shooting. Most YouTubers have a certain place that they generally shoot, but it usually takes a lot of trial and error to figure out the best location. In this chapter, we're going to look at ideas for the best background.

Some people keep the set design very simple: a solid color or green screen. If you're not familiar, a green screen is a screen that is colored and is a very specific tint of green. This color is random, based on the idea that people don't commonly wear it. Then, while you are editing the video, any instance of the green is taken out. You are left being able to put whatever you want in the background: a specific color, image, or animation. Green screens are not great for everyone, as they can be hard to manage with video editing, and do not provide the best look in certain situations. Regarding just a solid color, I usually do not recommend it. The video turns out a little bland and could use pictures or props.

When designing your set, you need to take your camera's capabilities (and how you want to use them) into mind. If you are looking for a blurry background, don't spend time adding precise detail. Instead, add interesting lights to make a cool effect. Additionally, add some colored furniture (or anything that could stand out). If you know that your lighting setup makes the foreground lighter than the background, try to keep your focus on the foreground.

Set design should not be random, and you need to try to stay on theme. If you are running a beauty channel, you should not have gaming posters in the background of your videos. Find props that make sense, and keep it consistent. Pick a prop that you know you can use for a long time, and keep it in the background until you need to switch it up. Your audience should be able to recognize your video just from the background, so make it unique.

No sets take up a whole room because there needs to be space for crew and equipment. When designing a set, make sure you make room for lighting. How lighting is placed is very important for proper set design. Green screens, for example, need very even lighting all around to avoid shadows (because shadows change the shade of green). Therefore, you should have three lights. One should be directly facing the subject, and the others should be on the left and right side at an angle. Lighting is always important, no matter what your scene. Proper lighting will even make the quality of the camera much better. Sometimes, one strong light (or the sun) can be enough. If you're using just one, make sure it's pointed right at you. If you want to make a harsh shadow on one side of your face, point the light perpendicular to the subject. Usually, simply adjusting the lights and checking the camera until it seems just right will do the trick.

Other than yourself, a set is the easiest way to display your personality to the viewers. Add things that you enjoy and make it unique. To test it out, check with family and friends to see if they believe it represents you. Also, remember that sets change, and you shouldn't *set* yourself on one design forever.

Conventions

The YouTube Community hosts many conventions and events throughout the year. Personally, I've only been to Vidcon, one of the biggest conventions, and it was a lot of fun. At Vidcon, I saw many large content creators like Phillip DeFranco, the Fine Brothers, Gabby Hanna, AsapScience (Mitchell Moffit and Gregory Brown), Matthias, Boogie2988, and many other inspiring YouTubers. Within just three days, I met incredible people, attended great panels, participated in fun activities, and had an overall wonderful time.

Vidcon is the first major convention for online content creators and has been going on for many years. It is definitely the first convention that comes to mind for many creators and is the most popular. Vidcon, started by John and Hank Green in 2010, hosts over 30,000 people per year. In 2017, they expanded Vidcon to around the world for many people to enjoy the festivities.

Vidcon has become a model for many other conventions. A typical day of Vidcon consists of many different events and a show-floor. On the show-floor, you can find an impressive number of different brands with booths displaying what they do. For example, in 2016, Musically had a small stage with performers and they gave away different prizes. Vidcon also has a few huge stages where more popular creators will host interviews and events.

If you purchase a creator or industry pass, you also get access to really cool "sessions." These sessions are interviews, panels, and Q&As with some really impressive people. For example, I went to a session about education on YouTube with asapScience. It is very exciting because you hear them talk, and then you can go out and chat with them.

Once you've made it big, you could become a "featured creator" at Vidcon. Featured creators have their hotel paid for and get full access to everywhere around Vidcon. Additionally, they get access to the most exclusive Vidcon parties and get-togethers. The requirements for becoming a featured creator are a bit unclear, but you need to be invited.

Playlist Live is an event that is quite similar to Vidcon, as it offers fan, creator, and business opportunities. All of their conventions are in the United States; they have been in Washington, D.C. and Orlando, Florida (locations might have changed). Playlist is one of the newer conventions but definitely showcases some really creative creators.

More into beauty and makeup? Beautycon is the number-one convention for that. In 2018, they will have conventions in New York, LA, and London. The great thing about a more specific convention is that you are truly surrounded by like-minded individuals.

RTX is the convention for all things gaming. Brought to you by the people from Rooster Teeth, RTX is an annual convention in Austin, Texas. After the three days of RTX, you will have been totally immersed in all things gaming. Sponsored by huge companies like Twitch, RTX is not a low-level convention and is a great time for the gaming community to shine.

Monetization Outside YouTube

If you are trying to make a living on YouTube, you need to rely on sources other than YouTube. Throughout this book, topics like affiliate programs are covered, but in this chapter, we'll go over some other great ways to monetize your content. Let me preface this chapter by saying that making money should not be a big focus for content creation, but for many, enables them to continue doing what they love.

One of the biggest platforms that help creators make money is Patreon.[15] Patreon lets your subscribers pledge a monthly donation (or a per-video) donation in exchange for perks. For example, you might post all your videos a week early on Patreon, and anyone willing to pay five dollars or more per month can see them. Patreon is a great tool that pays creators a lot of money, but you need to know how to approach it correctly. You need to make sure the perks are well worth it for your viewers. Some perk ideas are special credentials on a Discord server, access to early videos, weekly/monthly exclusive live-streams, behind the scenes content, merchandise discounts, and

---

[15] https://patreon.com/invite/xmrln

access to Patreon's built-in exclusive feed (where you can post videos, images, and content just for Patrons).

Merchandise is incredibly popular these days, as it's a great way for a viewer to represent a creator they enjoy. Merchandise can range from clothing to customized mugs or notebooks. The thing about merchandise, though, is that you need to be relatively popular to sell it well. Unlike Patreon, a customer usually only purchases merchandise once or twice. Additionally, you need to have a strong enough brand for someone to want to represent it in public. Though it seems complicated to set up, websites like Spreadshirt[16] can handle it all for you. Simply upload your design and share the link, and they'll pay you. Remember that you don't want to spam your viewers with too many of these off-YouTube Monetization tactics, so pick carefully.

Affiliate marketing is another great way to generate revenue and outlined later in a dedicated chapter. Affiliate marketing is where you are paid to promote a product, and paid every time one sells. Platforms like Amazon Associates[17] let you do this very easily, and you can even get paid in Amazon gift cards. Please visit the "Affiliate Programs" chapter to learn more about affiliate marketing.

Sponsorships and brand deals are probably the most popular ways to make money using your influence as a YouTube creator. Sponsorships aren't too easy to come by, as they require skill in communicating and working with companies. That said, if you know how to negotiate, the odds are in your favor. Getting a sponsorship is difficult without a very large amount of subscribers, but they can pay hundreds or thousands of dollars for one video. Even if you get one sponsor a month, it'll greatly

---

[16] https://www.spreadshirt.com/sell-merchandise

[17] https://affiliate-program.amazon.com/

affect your income. In a video, LinusTechTips[18] says that their company makes about 35% of their income from sponsors.

For some people, YouTube is just a way to sell products or services. If you are experienced enough with growing a YouTube channel, you could try selling consolation time to help others. If you're a writer, try writing a book and using your YouTube platform to help you sell it. In fact, you don't even need to be a writer to write a book (speaking from experience). If you're interested in going into this kind of business, you need to look into solutions for making a website and best delivery of your product/service, but it's definitely worth it.

---

[18] https://www.youtube.com/linustechtips

Consistency

At the beginning of the book, we discussed the YouTube algorithm and how it's ever-changing. One thing we've seen consistently favored is consistency. Consistency, or how often you upload content, is incredibly important for growing your channel. In this chapter, we'll discuss creating a schedule and the possibility of uploading daily.

A schedule is pretty straightforward and very important. Though the nice thing about being a YouTube creator is the creative freedom, it's also important to make a commitment to your viewers regarding when and how often you'll post. Figuring out your schedule can be difficult and should be done with a lot of thought and planning. When you come up with your schedule, you need to do everything you can to follow it.

There are two kinds of schedules you need to think of: production and publication. If you're a student with classes Monday through Friday, a schedule can be difficult, but not impossible. Let's also say that you have no free time during the week, and you want to post two videos a week. You may produce one video on Saturday and one on Sunday, and then use YouTube's Scheduling functionality to post them for the following week. Ideally, you want to post your videos spread out through the week, so maybe Monday and Thursday. You have now created both a production (Saturday/Sunday) and publication (Monday/Thursday) schedule.

It's difficult to accomplish, but it's very convenient to have a few video buffers. If you have a long weekend or some extra free time, make an additional video but don't post it yet. Also, don't let it interrupt your schedule, and keep making videos according to the plan. Now, in case you get sick or go on vacation, you have an extra video to post. If you know you'll be gone for a while, try to make as many videos as possible and spread them out throughout your time away.

Sticking to your schedule is also incredibly important, and you shouldn't have one if you can't stick to it. I know it can be challenging to feel motivated to create videos (see chapter entitled "Encouragement / Discouragement"), but it will break your rhythm to get out of a schedule. The more you break the routine, the easier it is to fall out of it.

Some have found that daily uploads are immensely beneficial and have seen incredible channel growth because of it. "Once I started uploading daily on my YouTube channel, everything changed. Engagement went up, and live-streams flourished. Most importantly my watch-time went through the roof. I went from 850 subscribers to 1.1k in two weeks," says Paul Groseclose[19], a content creator who uploaded every day for an entire month as a challenge. Though he posted videos for about two years prior to the challenge, he saw a remarkable and almost immediate growth.

Groseclose filled his week with five regular videos, a "question and answer" episode, and a live-stream. During this time, his community grew stronger and his analytics grew. Within a couple weeks, he had six people contributing a cash donation on a monthly basis via Patreon.

---

[19] https://www.youtube.com/channel/UCXohF8w0OMZZmd2IIoO64qw

Closed Captioning

For many people, closed captioning is just a button that is always an available option in the YouTube Player. But for some people, closed captioning (CC) is very important and the only way one might be able to fully watch YouTube. The deaf and hard-of-hearing community relies on proper CC. In addition, those who speak a different language, are trying to stay focused, or those watching without headphones will find CC to be a superior function.

You probably know by now that automatic closed captioning on YouTube is not very good. I mean, it is great for a computer. YouTube does what they can to turn your video into text. And sometimes, it does an incredible job, but not usually. For someone who relies on CC, "okay" is not good enough. In this chapter, we are going to go over the perks of CC your videos and the best ways to do them.

YouTube has a great solution for viewers to contribute CC. If you go into a specific video's editor page and select "Subtitles/CC," you can get started. Here, you can manually transcript your own video for closed captions, or find "community contributions." Make sure this is on, and it will allow any of your viewers to manually transcript the video.

PewDiePie[20], an incredibly popular YouTuber, can have over 70 viewers transcribe his videos into up to 20 languages. In return, they get a credit at the bottom of the description.

If you don't have that large of an audience, you should either do it manually or hire someone. Though I've never used specific services and cannot endorse any, I've seen many advertisements for $1/minute for captioning. Therefore, if you have a 4-minute video, you simply pay $4. Cannot afford it? As long as you are a fast or moderately fast typer, it shouldn't take too long to do it yourself.

There are several reasons why closed captioning your videos is important and beneficial. The first is a view boost. It is proven that videos with CC get more views, which lead to more engagement and subscriptions. Those who require CC can add that as a search filter (filter > features > subtitles/CC). As long as you have closed captioning on your video, it will show up with those filters applied. CC also helps with overall SEO (search engine optimization).

United Kingdom's Ofcom states that only about 20% of people using CC are actually deaf or hard of hearing. Although you may not fall into this category, it is very important to support the hard-of-hearing community. A deaf YouTuber by the name of Rikki Poynter[21] is a huge advocate for closed captioning on the YouTuber platform. She has personally made many videos about the importance of captioning and accessibility on the internet, and all of her videos are captioned.

Finally, closed captioning is important to many viewers with perfect hearing. Personally, I enjoy having closed captioning enabled on YouTube or on the television. If I'm watching with my family and they're chatting, I am still able to understand what is happening. When I'm in a busy place and

---

[20] youtube.com/pewdiepie

[21] youtube.com/user/rikkipoynter

don't have headphones (or don't feel comfortable blocking out the whole world), closed captioning can let me read what's on screen. For some, it just helps them focus a little bit more.

Intro's

There are a few things about your videos that are incredibly recognizable and stamp your brand on the video. One of those things is how you start each video, or your intro. It's a common misconception that an intro is a graphic display of your name or channel's name. For a while, honestly, I thought I needed that, too. In reality, though, your intro is simply the series of events that start your video.

A saying like, "top of the morning to you laddies[22]" or "hi fellas and girls[23]" is the most common first "event" found in a video. I, personally, find this saying to be incredibly important but also incredibly hard to come by. It's difficult to find a saying that's unique and properly utilizes your voice. For example, "top of the mornin' to you laddies," an Irish saying, is said by JackSepticEye, an Irish Gamer. Some people jump right into the video without a saying and are able to do it very well. That said, it's hard to perfect. The intro is a nice intro the content itself, and some people need it to be able to make their video properly. Whatever you do: keep it consistent.

---

[22] http://youtube.com/jacksepticeye

[23] https://www.youtube.com/user/thiskidneedsmedicine, Grandma Lill

Let's go back and discuss the graphic intro. I've seen that a lot of smaller content creators use cheesy, loud, long, and overused graphic clips at the beginning of their videos. Usually, though, it's not the right route to go down. The mood of each video is very different, and having a set graphic intro is not able to properly match that. With the previous case regarding the saying, you are able to say this in a very different tone. Here's my checklist for a *proper* graphic intro:

- Short, under five seconds. (If I get *bored* of watching your intro, I'm definitely not watching the video itself.)
- No overused animation, maybe just your channel name printed nicely.
- Not being played as the first frame, but implementing it into a few seconds of dialogue.
- Staying constant—don't change it every day.
- Make it aesthetically pleasing!
- The music shouldn't be much louder than the rest of the video.
- Make it look nice! (Again, to show emphasis.)
- Suggestion, not a requirement: Don't have the graphic include audio, but instead use that of the video. This way, it feels less like a complete cutaway from the video and more of an integration. Also, you now have control over the mood.
- *Make it look nice!*

As you can see, there's a lot that I look for in a high-quality intro. I genuinely believe that they are unnecessary, but if you are able meet all of these requirements, it's definitely a nice add-on. A lot of creators starting out find "intro generators" or other over-to-top means of creating an intro, but it's simple: add a background color to the frame, add your channel name or logo, change the font to something that fits your brand, and (if you can) animate the text onto the screen and add a subtle sound effect.

    The last part of your intro is your body movement and actions. This part isn't as important as the others, but you're going to want to keep an eye out. Going back to JackSepticEye, he always high-fives the air with a whipping sound effect before saying "top of the mornin' to you laddies." This half-second motion is yet another way of associating the start of the video with one's brand. Whether it be a small wave, high-five, head-bob, or other motion, it's important that you add a bit of movement to your opening scene. Not only does the movement help create an association with your brand, it just simply helps you loosen up a little bit before diving into the video. Again, don't obsess over a little movement, but you don't want to stand stiff while trying to captivate an audience (the beginning is the best time to draw them in).

Banner Design

It doesn't seem like the biggest deal, but banner design is very important for your channel's branding. Your banner shows up on your channel on all platforms: mobile, desktop, and even TV. In fact, some may argue that TV is the most important place for your banner because it's so large and is a main focus. Designing your banner takes time, effort, and a lot of creative ability. It's also important to make sure your banner stays updated and accurate.

YouTube has a collection of random pictures that you can use for your banner, but I do not recommend them. A random picture might look cool, but it gives viewers no information about your channel and sometimes looks a bit lazy. Even if you aren't a professional graphic designer, there are better options and many tools that can help you.

The first thing you want to keep in mind while designing your banner is your channel icon. The channel icon is featured on top of your banner, so make sure you don't put important content in a place that'll be covered by the icon. The icon is overlaid near the top left corner, so steer away from text or pictures in that area. Additionally, you might want to match the color scheme of the banner with the icon.

YouTube provides very specific dimensions and requirements for a banner, but they also provide a nice template[24] with all the dimensions outlined. If you're using a dedicated website to help you make a YouTube banner, you should have these dimensions already in mind. Generally, though, the image should be 2560x1440px and smaller than six megabytes.

But what do you put on your banner? That's a great question, and it really depends. Obviously, you need to make sure the banner fits your niche and the topic of your channel. There are two routes you can go: real images or graphic design. Down the "real images" route, a makeup channel might have images of makeup with the channel name on top. Down the "graphic design" route, a makeup channel might have the name of the channel graphically presented and added images like makeup emojis or something recognizable. In the end, you want the banner to represent what you do on your channel and have it look aesthetically pleasing.

Ideally, you want someone to be able to look at your channel banner and have them know exactly what your channel is about. Whether the banner explicitly says it or uses images to convey the message is up to you. That said, only displaying your channel name with a solid background color is not enough. You also want it to look nice, as it's usually a first impression when someone visits your channel.

As I said before, the banner will be viewed on a range of screens—from phones to TVs—so you need to make sure everything is readable from different sizes. If your text or images are too small, viewers won't be able to see the banner and are less likely to subscribe.

---

[24] https://goo.gl/13Tgg1

Here is my personal checklist when designing a banner:

- Take a step back and squint: Can you still (mostly) understand it?
- Minimize the window to the size of a phone or tablet; Can you still read it?
- Hide the name on the banner and have someone else look at it. Are they able to tell it's for your channel? Remember that your banner should match the branding and the feel of your content.
- Do research on similar channels—do they use a similar layout? Try to stand out!
- Is the banner blurry and hard to read? Try editing the resolution or using a different software.
- Are you only using images that you have legal rights to use? (Yeah, that matters.)

Longer Videos

Recently, people have been questioning whether or not the YouTube algorithm prefers longer videos. Some find that videos over 10 minutes have performed better and shown more ads, where some find it's unnecessary to drag a video out that long. In this chapter, we'll go over the pros and cons and look into enabling your channel for uploading videos over 15 minutes.

Back in July of 2016, creators started to figure out the benefits of uploading videos over 10 minutes. Even if the video was a second over 10 minutes, creators would see incredible benefits. YouTube would start showing more ads, they'd see more views, and experience more financial gain. In fact, YouTube even encourages uploads over 10 minutes because it provides them with more hours of content available on their platform. So, that sounds all good, then what's the downside?

Ten minutes is a long time for a single YouTube video. Not only does it take a longer time to record, edit, and publish, but the attention span of a typical viewer is usually much shorter than 10 minutes. When viewers see a 10-minute video, they are more likely to leave at the first sign of restlessness than a shorter video. Therefore, the video itself needs to be longer, but there's a larger requirement to make it entertaining the entire time. So as a creator, making a ten-minute video is much harder.

Another important consideration when looking into creators taking advantage of the 10-minute benefits is quality. It's unavoidable, but some YouTuber's are just in it for the money. (If that's your mindset, you need to either stop or reevaluate.) Creators will start making videos unnecessarily long and the overall quality of their content will just fall. Additionally, they'll leave in breaks and takes that they would usually cut out. If you are trying to make longer videos, which I totally support, remember: The quality of the content is much more important than the quantity and length.

If you are looking to make a video over 15 minutes long, there's a certain process you need to go through. You need to make sure your account is verified, which you can do at youtube.com/verify, and then you're good to go! Until you do this, there's a 15-minute limit on your uploads. Also, make sure your browser allows uploads over 20 gigabytes, as that will be necessary when uploading very lengthy videos.

Just a heads up: The maximum upload is 12 hours or 128gb, whichever is less. That said, there should be no reason for an upload that large. Think about how much your average viewer will watch, and try not to spam your viewer's subscription feeds with obnoxiously long videos.

So just to sum all of this up, long videos may be beneficial but shouldn't be forced. If you are able to keep the viewer engaged for 10 minutes and you are able to take on the challenge, you should do so. If you have any doubts, try it once or twice, but don't force it. Not everything that can be done should be done.

MCNs and Networks

A YouTube Network, or MCN (Multi-Channel Network), is a company that manages multiple YouTube channels. These companies are not run by YouTube and can offer many perks to different creators, but they do charge a fee. There are many different MCNs that a YouTube channel could sign with that do very different things.

Instead of having ad revenue flow into your AdSense account, it flows into your network's account, and the network pays you. Additionally, they provide you with extra help, access to paid platforms, and other tools. What's the catch? They usually take anywhere from ten to forty percent of your earnings in return for their services. In this chapter, we're going to compare some of the top networks, and if networks are worth it.

Personally, I've only been with a network for a little bit of my YouTube career. In fact, I managed a network and had a lot of fun doing that. Unfortunately, YouTube changed their policies about sub-networks and I was forced out of the business. Other than the time I was linked to my own network, I have spent about three months in a network. The services are incredible and the support is great, but a 35% cut is a lot. Say I make fifty dollars from ads on YouTube. A whopping 45% of that amount goes to YouTube (which is unavoidable—network or not), and then 35% goes to the network. Then, I take-home only $17.87 (50 x 0.55 x 0.65). Therefore, I take home 35.75% of ad revenue versus the traditional 55%.

For someone who doesn't make a whole lot of money on YouTube, a 35% cut can make small revenue even smaller. Also, not many networks will give too much attention to a smaller channel, so you get their basic perks. Standard perks include access to paid software for background music, access to their forums, and customer support. (Just a little tip: networks will always brag about their customer support. Always ask yourself: how often will I need a question answered, and how much is that worth?)

Once I was in a network, I realized I was really only using their dashboard because it looked better than the YouTube dashboard. I wasn't utilizing many of their tools or their customer service. So for me, it definitely wasn't worth 35% to join a network. That said, I keep my eyes open for a better deal and better services.

If you are having second thoughts, remember that MCNs aren't for everyone, and for most people, it doesn't make financial sense to join one. Most popular content creators will join one because they will help with bigger-picture things, but for small to medium sized channels, it's a tough sell.

Name of the Network	Typical Revenue Share	Top Services
Scalelab	65%	- Forums - Support - Medium tier apps
Fullscreen Media	70%	- Creator Platform - Help with touring/meet-ups - Management
BBTV	60%	- Creator Platform - Medium Tier Apps
Freedom	60%	- No lock-in contract - Medium tier apps - No payout threshold
Maker Studios / RPM	60%	- Forums - Medium tier apps
iFree	70%	- No lock-in contract
MediaCube	80%	- Distribute your music - High tier apps

Keep in mind that networks will offer different creators different revenue shares based on popularity, but the "Typical Revenue Share" is usually the minimum.

SEO

Search Engine Optimization, or SEO, occurs all over the internet. With every search engine, like Bing, Google, YouTube, or Yahoo, there are many algorithms in place to figure out what shows up and in what order. Most of the time, the exact algorithm is private, but SEO is a series of things you can do to increase your chances of appearing higher. YouTube and Google aren't the only search engines that can bring traffic to your videos, as other search engines and websites can bring a great amount of attention to your channel. In this chapter, we will explore the best ways to properly optimize your videos and channel for search engines.

Tags are incredibly important for getting proper attention. When you upload a video, you need to make sure you are adding as many quality tags as you can think of. Add different word variations of related information. For example, in a video about the iPhone X, add tags like "iPhone," "iPhone x," "iPhone 10," "iPhone ten," "Apple," "Apple iPhone," "Apple iPhone X." As you can see, I have entered all the variations of iPhone X, and added other relevant tags, like "Apple." Make sure to keep your tags on topic, though. This way, the search engine can show your content when a user searches different variations.

Though it's something you can't completely control, engagement is incredibly important. Factors like views, comments, likes, and watch-time definitely influence the algorithm. Stay active in the comment section to increase the number of comments and encourage others to leave comments. Also, make your videos interesting and fast-paced to increase viewers' watch-time.

Let's chat a little more about promoting your video. Promoting your video does a few different things. Not only does it increase one-time views and comments, but it can lead to long-term subscribers. For SEO, it does two great things. It increases the popularity of the video and shows YouTube that the video is being shared (because they track the location of traffic). You can promote your video on social media, in your email signature, in person, or via online forums. But be careful: you don't want to mindlessly post links to your video on the internet, because you will quickly be blocked from websites and forums. Post them in context or with another response. If someone asks a question on a website and you have a video about it—great, promote! If you are submitting a response and have the link in your signature—great, promote! Don't make a new post just about the video if it's not warranted. You should be confident enough with your videos to share them with friends and people you know offline.

"Titles and descriptions" have their own dedicated chapter, but we're going to touch on them briefly here. Search engines will do their best to determine if the titles and descriptions are of high quality. A low-quality title will heavily weigh down your video in a search engine. A bad title is less "clickable," and search engines are trying to get as many clicks as possible. For a high-quality title, make sure you use proper capitalization, proper punctuation, and avoid clickbait. Clickbait is when a title and thumbnail mislead the viewer regarding the contents of the video. Sure, they might get you some extra views, but search engines and viewers hate clickbait. Also, pick a keyword and put that at the beginning of the title. For example, "**iPhone X** Review and Unboxing" is better than "Unboxing and Review of the **iPhone X**." Make sure this keyword ("iPhone X") also appears at least twice in the description to show importance.

There are many different factors that go into a successful video, but discovery is one of the most important. Since discovery is backed by SEO, it is important that you don't ignore it. There are certain tools, like TubeBuddy,[25] that will add a checklist next to the upload page with helpful tips and tricks. Surveying subscribers to make sure videos are going out and easy to discover is important feedback to collect and analyze.

---

[25] tubebuddy.com/ythandbook

YouTube Space

YouTube Space gives incredible opportunities to content creators. Personally, I have not experienced YouTube Space but would love to someday (if only they opened one in Chicago). YouTube has opened these hugely impressive buildings around the world. For example, YouTube Space LA is 44,000 square feet and is built in an old airport. Inside these buildings, there are so many innovative things to experience. They have top-of-the-line equipment for you to use for free, in addition to seminars, events, groups and more. As of the beginning of 2018, there are eight locations worldwide (including LA, London, Rio, and Tokyo), but more are opening.

"Unlocking the space" is a required process to be able to make content at YouTube Space. These are the required steps for the LA space, but it's pretty similar everywhere else. To start, you must have 10,000 subscribers and no copyright strikes or problems with your account. If you're under 18, you need to be accompanied by an adult. The process of "unlocking the space" isn't too extensive. Start by participating in a one-hour online training. Next, participate in a live session that goes into more depth and sign the terms of conditions.

Once you've unlocked the space, you have access to a ton of benefits. In Space LA, a channel under 100,000 subscribers has access to a small stage for one day per month and three days of post-production per month. That said, they have full access to gear trainings, special events, open houses, and more. As you gain subscribers, you unlock more (and bigger) stage days, host events at Space, and have their live-streams engineered.

YouTube Space gives you many opportunities, so isn't there a catch? Not really. Before publishing any content that you've made at Space, it must be reviewed. It must meet copyright and community guidelines. Otherwise, there's no fee or strings attached. Also, if you're planning your visit, remember that YouTube provides equipment but not a crew. Bring some of your friends to help you film and produce your videos.

One of the coolest things are the different groups that you can join. They're kind of like clubs in high school, as anyone can make a request to start one and there are so many out there. These groups can help you meet other individuals that are like you and make similar content. Some groups include LGBTQ, Vegan, Comedy, Asian Creators, Musicians. Each meeting of the group may bring something new, but you can expect networking, socialization, lessons, and workshops.

If you ever have a chance to visit or utilize YouTube Space, take the opportunity! The building and design itself is beautiful and the community is even better. Even before you hit 10,000 subscribers, you have access to open houses, community events, boot camps, and more. To learn more, you can visit: youtube.com/yt/space.

Demonetization

Demonetization was briefl mentioned in the "monetization" chapter, but here's we're going to go into a little more detail. It all started in March 2017, when advertisers realized their ads were going next to inappropriate and extremist videos. Advertisers didn't want to be associated with that kind of content and stopped purchasing ads on YouTube. Some companies that pulled advertisements included the UK Government, Coca-Cola, and Dr. Pepper (to name a few). A couple of months later, Pepsi released an advertisement featuring Kendall Jenner, where she resolved a protest by handing the police a can of Pepsi. The world went mad, and Pepsi ended up pulling all of their advertising from YouTube because of the public outcry.

Then began the *adpocalypse* in the summer of 2017. Fewer and fewer companies were advertising on YouTube and creators were making very little. To try to win advertisers back, YouTube only enabled ads on videos that were considered "advertiser-friendly." Even more outrage came from this because many videos were demonetized altogether. Throughout the summer, YouTube creators were becoming more and more conscious about inappropriate content and explicit language.

Since an algorithm started automatically demonetizing videos, some videos would be demonetized with no reason at all.

As of the beginning of 2018, very little has changed. Advertisers have slowly come back, but videos are still being demonetized. In fact, I've had a couple videos demonetized for no reason at all. All of my videos are family friendly with no harsh language or imagery at all. Many people submit requests for manual reviews to get videos monetized again, but there are requirements. YouTube requires that your video have over 1,000 views in the last seven days to submit a manual review request. Since neither of these videos meets that condition, there is nothing I can do.

There are two ways that a video on YouTube makes money: ads and YouTube Red. If your video is demonetized, ads will not be shown and you lose that revenue. Demonetized videos will still generate revenue from YouTube Red. That's great and all, but YouTube Red revenue usually accounts for less than 10% of total revenue. Creators are very upset because this demonetization algorithm is tanking up to 90% of revenue from them with little to no reasoning.

Though YouTube hasn't commented on it, many content creators complain of "video suppression." They claim that when their video becomes demonetized, it also doesn't show up in sub boxes and the number of viewers goes down. Jon Prosser[26], a technology reporter whose show is commonly demonetized, has evidence that video suppression is real and harsh. At one point, Jon says that his show, Front Page Tech (FPT), was demonetized every single day for months—usually before being fully uploaded. Jon Prosser writes:

> There's really no hard evidence behind it, but it's hard to ignore it when you can watch the suppression happen in real time. It seems that if you upload a video, monetized,

---

[26] youtube.com/user/frontpagetech

and at some point, it gets demonetized by the flagging system, that same system also places some sort of restriction on the video. My guess is that videos don't get suppressed because they aren't monetized, they're getting suppressed for *why* they were demonetized. Maybe it's considered inappropriate, therefore YouTube doesn't rank it as high or recommend it as much? There's no doubt, though, that when we upload a video and it gets flagged as 'not suitable for all advertisers,' everything takes a hit -- our views are cut down by 70% -- it's a very noticeable impact. We've also seen videos get re-monetized and suddenly, views [on] the real-time graphs shoot up. Suppression is happening, and YouTube isn't being transparent. This shouldn't be guess-work.

Encouragement / Discouragement

In this chapter, we will dive a little deeper than most other chapters. Being encouraged and then discouraged about content creation can happen very easily. For me, I go through months of not making a video because of many different reasons. We're going to explore some of the more common reasons and how you can stay motivated.

One of the most common reasons that a small creator may get discouraged is because of rude comments or harassment. When you expose yourself to the world by creating a video and making it public, you don't expect you are going to get negative attention, but it happens. And sure, it's easy to respond back with mean comments or just delete them altogether, but that's not always ideal. You can't fight fire with fire, so responding to mean comments is never prudent. Additionally, a comment with a response (let alone a response from the video creator) appears higher in the comment section. Therefore, responding to mean comments would result in the comment appearing higher in the comment section, and even more people viewing it. So why wouldn't you just delete the comment? You want to be transparent and to make sure that any member of your audience gets a chance to state their opinion. Don't try to censor other people.

Try to think to yourself about how little this stranger means to you, and how they weren't able to tell you in person. Sometimes, you need to take criticism and actually make that change. They could be trying to just bring you down, but use the criticism to help you get stronger.

Another reason a lot of new content creators get discouraged is the lack of views or subscribers. Sometimes you might feel that you worked really hard on a video and almost nobody watched it. I feel that on YouTube, we put too much value in the numbers. The main reason you should be making videos is for your own pleasure—not to be obsessed with views. That said, it is understandable to feel disappointed after releasing a video that doesn't do as well. Let's say that I am down about a video that only got 50 views. To feel better, I close my eyes and imagine a room. In this room, there are 50 people. A number that seemed minuscule a second ago suddenly seems large. 50 views may not seem like a lot until you imagine 50 people.

One way you can stay encouraged is making goals. Let's say you really want to hit 100 subscribers by the end of the year. To reach this goal, you are going to need to work hard and make content. And if you don't make the goal, extend it by a couple of months. To get these subscribers, you'll need to make quality content, interact with the community, and stay encouraged. Do things like making a countdown on a whiteboard to keep the goal in your head. The most important thing to staying motivated is making sure that you're having fun throughout the entire process.

YouTube is very faced-paced and you might feel like you need to be working on your channel 24/7, but that will lead to burnout. Make sure you fit in other things, like social interactions, and don't spend too much time on one video. Maybe record one day and edit the next. If it feels too much like a chore, you take the fun out of it and you'll start to get discouraged.

At some point, you will get discouraged and that's unavoidable. Sometimes, it's healthy to take up to a couple of months off to relight the spark. Everything will be there when you get back, but maybe you'll have a few more views and subscribers. Eric Drinkard from Creator of the Week comments:

> One of the hardest parts of being a creator is keeping the motivation up. Not too many people start their online career with a massive following and it is something that takes time to grow. Here is the thing though, you can't give up. If this is your passion, if this is what you want to do for a living, then you have to keep going. The moment you give up, that is the moment you failed. Learn to adapt and take criticism without changing who you are. Many fellow creators will tell you that the market is saturated. This is all how you look at the problem. This is where being different than the rest will help you. Take the time to look at your competition, read the comments on your videos. Then take a step back, reevaluate and push forward. Most importantly no matter what KEEP CREATING.

Affiliate Programs

Affiliate programs are the easiest way to subtly make a few extra dollars from your videos. Here's how it works: Tom's Toys says that if you advertise their products, they will pay you 5% of everything you sell. Unlike an advertisement, you don't get paid a predetermined amount. In one video, you shout-out their website and some of your viewers buy products from Tom's Toys. The total of what your viewers bought was $100, so you take home $5 (5% of $100). This is beneficial for both you and Tom because you can make some money, and Tom gets more sales.

Affiliate marketing is nothing new on YouTube and is literally everywhere. And when I say that, I'm not exaggerating. Any video that has a link to a product in the description is most likely an affiliate link. Every time a creator tells you to use a referral code or go to a special link, that is usually an affiliate link (sometimes it's just sponsored). Affiliate marketing is super simple and there's no reason you shouldn't get started. I make an effort to add my affiliate code to all the Amazon links I post (or send to friends and family). Then, I get random $10 gift cards from Amazon every couple of months for doing almost nothing.

There are many, many different affiliate programs out there, but the most popular is Amazon Associates[27] (AA). AA gives you up to 8.5% commission on any Amazon product. This offers many different uses to make a quick buck. If you create makeup videos, you can link all of the products used in the video to your affiliate link. Then, if one of your viewers bought any of those products, you get paid.

Personally, I try to use AA as much as possible. In the description of all of my videos, I have affiliate links to all of my gear. Additionally, if I mention a product in the video, I will link it. I don't make a lot of money from AA, but I do get paid a few dollars here and there. Pro tip: Sharing an affiliate link "endorses" it, so make sure you are confident with the product because your reputation is on the line.

Affiliate marketing is literally everywhere on YouTube. iJustine[28], a technology YouTuber, promotes a game called HQ Trivia[29] to get extra lives. She is not paid to do so and has no direct connection to the company. Anybody can take advantage of their "invite a friend" program, but she is using her platform. Another example is with Uber. Uber has many promotions where individuals can get hundreds of dollars by referring others to use their service. Some channels, like RideShare Tips[30], make hundreds of dollars weekly (sometimes more) just by referring people to Uber. Again, anyone is able to do this, but they are using their platform.

Regarding the Federal Trade Commission (FTC), you should be disclosing any affiliate links or programs that you are participating in. The rules are much more strict for straight-up sponsored content, but you should stay safe. The FTC website

---

[27] www.affiliate-program.amazon.com

[28] youtube.com/user/ijustine

[29] www.hqtrivia.com

[30] youtube.com/channel/UCIdEYx5MwpISAujYA6cwvWg

says that for affiliate links, simply putting "(affiliate link")" next to the link or code should be enough. Remember that the FTC wants viewers to be aware and not tricked into anything.

Copyright

Copyright is one of my favorite chapters to write about because there's so much information and so much misconception. Just a quick preface: this information is based on United States law. That said, it's similar to other law, and this is the law YouTube goes by. If you abide by the guidelines covered in this chapter, you shouldn't face problems. First: what is copyright? Let's say that I write a book. Then, some random person comes across my book, copies it word-for-word, publishes it, and then makes a lot of money off of it. According to copyright laws, this is illegal. Copyright prevents making money off of other's people's work. But, there are some exceptions.

How does this pertain to YouTube? Well, it happens a lot. If you are using background music in your video, most likely you don't have written permission from the artist. Some artists will say "anyone can use my music," and that's called royalty-free, but most popular songs are not this way. Then, as you make money from your video, you are also making money from the artist's work—which is unfair. But what if I'm not making money from my YouTube channel? Well, you still didn't get permission from the artist, and the music is being distributed without them getting paid, so it's an infringement of copyright.

YouTube manages copyright so carefully because they could get sued if they didn't. If they let anything slide, and then an artist sued a creator for copyright infringement, YouTube might get in trouble for being the distributor. In fact, in 2010, Viacom International sued YouTube for this very reason. The case was overturned and still remains pending.

It's not only music. Any work of art that you did not make yourself is subject to copyright. Some examples include pulling clips from TV shows or movies (or even someone else's YouTube video), pictures, and even written work (like a poem). When you upload your video to YouTube, it automatically checks the background of the video for any copyrighted material. If it finds any, you won't be able to make money from that video. If an artist personally submits a claim against your video, they could even take it down. Though it's annoying, YouTube does this to protect you and themselves from a lawsuit.

Fair use is one of the biggest misconceptions regarding copyright law since the law makes it so unclear. Fair use states that some works of copyright may be used without permission. If you are making a parody or commenting on something, then you are protected by fair use. Be careful, as "commenting" is very unclear. If you are making a reaction video and showing the video in the corner, but not making many reactions, you could be in trouble. With a parody, there needs to be a strong difference between your version and theirs. If you change one little thing, you may not be protected.

One of the worst things I see is when someone uploads a song or clip of a movie, doesn't modify it, and claims fair use in the description. With fair use, you need to show clearly that you made modifications. A big misconception is that you can legally use 15 or 30 seconds of a song legally. That is not true at all. You can get in trouble for a even few seconds of a song if the artist wants to take action.

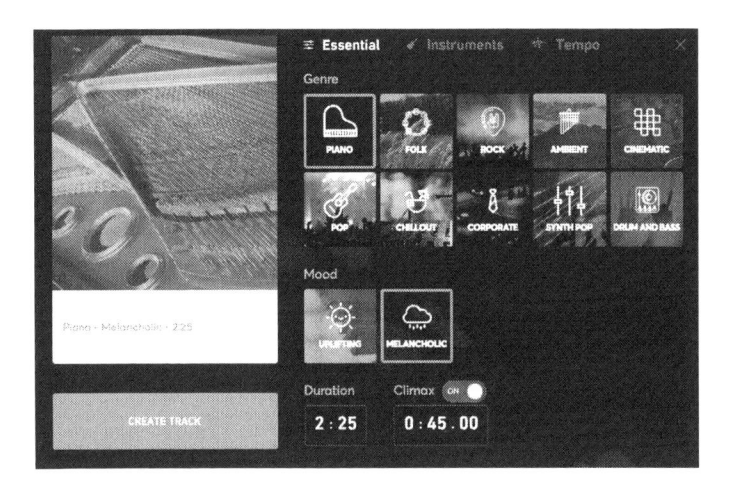

I use a program called Jukedeck[31] for all of my music. It allows you to input a bunch of different conditions about a song, and then uses artificial intelligence to create it. Every song is different and sounds great. As long as you put a link in the description to their site, it's completely free and you won't get in trouble with the law.

To avoid getting your channel shut down or getting sued, make sure you only use materials in your videos that you made or you got permission to use. If you want to learn more about copyright, YouTube provides great resources[32].

---

[31] www.jukedeck.com

[32] https://www.youtube.com/yt/about/copyright/#learn-about-copyright

Responding to Comments

Responding to comments might be one of the easiest ways to make your audience stronger. You'll see a lot of channels will try to respond to as many comments in the first 30 minutes as possible. Therefore, they are encouraging people to watch the video soon (so they won't forget about it) and encouraging them to write a comment. Regarding the YouTube algorithm, comments do play a part. It's not huge, but it definitely shows engagement from the audience.

When someone gets a response from the creator, even if they're not super popular, it starts to break the wall between creator and viewer. It makes the creator feel more like a person and not just somebody behind the camera.

Here's what you can do to respond to a comment:

Type a Response: Though it is the easiest, typing a response can show the most personalized effect on a viewer. The most common reply is "thank you" or "thanks" in response to a positive comment. If you made a how-to video and somebody asked a question, definitely answer it! I've made how-to videos before and gotten questions on YouTube, Instagram, and Twitter. **Do not** respond to negative or spam comments. Responding to a comment will move it up on the comments feed, and you only want nice things up there. You *can* delete comments, but sometimes you just need to ignore them.

Pinning a Comment: By clicking the three vertical dots near a comment, you will see this menu. This menu has four great tools for handling comments. We'll be focusing on "pin." The pin function came out near the end of 2016 and can do many things. It literally pins a comment to the top of the comment section. You can only pin one comment per video, though. In the past, I've used it to pin a comment of my own to thank people for watching and to like and subscribe. Some creators also pin a comment from themselves linking to another video that a view should watch. The last way it can be used is pinning a funny or nice comment about the video. If the first comment is a nice one, it could boost the tone throughout the entire comment section.

"Heart" a Comment: Hearting a comment may just be the easiest way to respond because it just requires one click. Sure, it doesn't feel as personal, but viewers certainly appreciate a heart. As the creator of the video, every comment will have a little heart next to the typical reply, thumbs up, and thumbs down options. If you decide that you would like to "heart" a comment, simply select the heart button. Then, next to the comment will be your profile picture and a little heart. Doing this means very little, but it shows the commenter that you appreciate the comment.

Additionally, it could increase the chance that the comment would appear higher up in the comment section.

Benefit Levels

YouTube splits channels into four categories, or levels, based on the number of subscribers they have. Each of these levels has different benefits when it comes to what YouTube can provide to you. Each level has a different amount of support they receive from YouTube and different opportunities.

Graphite: Once you get your first subscriber and until you get your 1000th subscriber, you are a Graphite creator. Graphite creators are not eligible for many perks, as it is the lowest and default level. So sure, YouTube doesn't open up many doors until you hit quadruple digits, but they still help you out. As a Graphite creator, you have access to a lot of training content about how to grow your channel and succeed on the platform. In addition, you can opt-in to receive "Creator Monthly," a monthly newsletter about YouTube news, opportunities, and events. During your time in the Graphite level, it is a great idea to start to understand copyright. As you post your first few videos, it's super easy to think "YouTube won't care if I use a copy-written song in my videos," but they do! The YouTube system doesn't care about your numbers when it comes to copyright infringements. Then, there's the Newbie Room. The Newbie Room is a forum moderated by YouTube only for

Graphite channels. You can read a lot about other creators, ask questions to the community, and more.

Opal: Congrats on hitting 1,000 subscribers! Until you hit 10,000, you are an Opal channel. Opal channels have a lot more options and perks. You can start by attending YouTube-sponsored meet-ups. You can talk to like-minded individuals and have a lot of fun. You now qualify for certain events at YouTube Space and can attend workshops, happy hours, music nights, screenings, and more. Though you might not yet qualify to join YouTube Space for production, you can attend events. Well, you probably get the theme: events. Now, you can join a creator day—a fun-packed day (each a little different) filled with panels, conversations, and more. Sounds fun! As an Opal channel, you have access to the Events Room. You can talk to other Opal channels about events (online and in real life).

Bronze: 10,000 subscribers—wow! Now, until you get your Silver Play Button (100,000 subscribers), you are a Bronze creator. Since few people achieve this rank, even more doors open up for you. Let's talk personalization. You can be connected with a YouTube partner manager to personally help you one-time with your channel. You now have a contact on the inside of YouTube that can help with everything! YouTube Space is now unlocked. You can walk into a YouTube Space building (many are located around the world), and use YouTube's equipment to record videos on sets, edit, host your now events, and so much more! It's an experience any creator dreams of. As a Bronze channel, you have access to the Tricks and Tips Room. You can talk to other Bronze channels about tips and tricks when it comes to YouTube.

Silver and Up: Welcome to the top! Silver creators have 100,000 subscribers and more. By entering this level, you receive your Silver play button and are on track for gold and diamond. Remember the YouTube Partner from Bronze? Well, they are now even more dedicated to you. You can work with them as much as you want about much more advanced channel details (like business/creative strategies). Have you ever been to a YouTube party with only famous YouTubers? No? Well, now you can. Check your inbox, because throughout the year you will receive invites to exclusive parties. Also, you get the top level of access to YouTube Space. As a Silver and up channel, you have access to the Community News Room. You can read updates about the happenings of YouTube.

YouTube Studio App

The YouTube Studio app, available on both the App Store and Google Play Store, is an incredible resource for monitoring your channel on the go. Personally, I use it to respond to comments, view basic analytics, and edit the title or description of a video. If you're a creator, the app is a great tool to manage your channel on-the-go and is a no-brainer.

When you open the app, you are presented with your dashboard. This includes basic analytical data: watch-time, views, subscriber change, and estimated revenue in the last 28 days, with comparison to the data of the previous 28 days. Next, you are presented with your three most recent videos, their title, thumbnail, view count, comment count, like count, privacy setting, and monetization status. Finally, you can see your three most recent comments.

So, as you can see, by just quickly opening up the app, you gain important information about your channel. But, there's a lot more. At the top of the main menu, you can easily switch between different channels. In the main menu, you have some options: dashboard, videos, playlists, comments, analytics, and more.

Each page is very detailed and really could do a lot of things that the desktop creator studio can do. In the video tab, you can edit the thumbnail, title, description, privacy, tags, monetization, category, age restrictions, comment/like blocking, and more. In addition, you can delete a video. This has become very useful for me to check to make sure my video is monetized, change the privacy to public, and even change the thumbnail.

One of my favorite features is the comments page. When you get a lot of comments, it's very convenient to be able to respond to them all from your phone. You can view your most recent comments (that are separated by video), respond, like, report, delete, and report them.

The analytics tab has as much information as the desktop version but is much easier to read and understand. Simple data, such as watch-time and viewers are available, but so is advanced data, like "Clicks per card shown" and "Top videos suggesting your content." All of these are shown in color-coordinated graphs and tables.

The YouTube Studio app allows you to be notified with new comments on your channel. You can switch between all comments, important comments, and no comments. For a small channel that doesn't get many comments, this can be great so you can quickly respond! For medium or larger sized channels, you can turn on "important comments" and be notified by a very popular comment, or comment by a popular channel. Either way, it's great to quickly respond to comments and be in-the-know.

So, whether you get 10 views on a video or 10 million, the YouTube Studio app is a great resource to quickly check up on comments and make quick modifications.

Fair Use Statement

The YouTuber's Handbook was made without direct permission from YouTube, Google, Alphabet, or any other brands. Though permission was requested through YouTube's Brand Use resources, there was no response.

The use of "YouTube" and other copy-written content throughout this book is in compliance with Section 107 of the United States[33] Copyright Act, *fair use*.

"Criticism, comment, news reporting, teaching, scholarship, and research"[34] qualify as fair use. Due to the fact that this book is commenting on the YouTube platform, reporting on changes, teaching people about the platform, and contains a large amount of opinion and original content, we are protected by this act.

At no point in this book do we take business away from YouTube or slander the company's name, but instead help increase the quality of creators and, in turn, increase profit for YouTube and other brands mentioned. We have made it clear on the back cover and inside that this book is not created by YouTube, therefore not confusing customers looking for YouTube-created content. Someone buying this book will not monetarily hurt YouTube, Google, or Alphabet.

We only use the logo on the front cover, which is still protected by fair use. Again, we provide a clear disclaimer regarding the rights to the logo and the name. If you feel your copyright has been violated in this book, please contact legal@oliverleopold.com.

---

[33] This book was written, published, and distributed in the United States. Alphabet is a US business.

[34] https://www.copyright.gov/fair-use/more-info.html, accessed 5/27/2018

Oliver Leopold is an American author from Evanston, Illinois. His various interests include technology, the internet, content creation, programming, and writing. In 2015, he wrote the first edition of *The YouTuber's Handbook*, and now believes it's ready for an update. Oliver Leopold was a 15-years-old high school freshman when he wrote this book, and he hopes to discover even more about the YouTube platform as it grows and changes. Oliver has a YouTube channel himself with over 6,000 subscribers (as of early 2018), and juggles all of his interests and projects. In his free time, Oliver is hired to make websites, write code, create videos, and more. Though he doesn't want to become a professional pilot, Oliver is working towards his pilot's license for enjoyment and fun. Oliver lives in Evanston, IL with his family, two rescue dogs, and parrot, Maxwell.

Manufactured by Amazon.ca
Bolton, ON